6 Ways for Men to Thrive in Midlife

Stephen Arterburn

AspirePress

Peabody, Massachusetts

AspirePress

6 Ways for Men to Thrive in Midlife
Copyright © 2017 Stephen Arterburn
All rights reserved.
Aspire Press is an imprint of Hendrickson Publishers Marketing, LLC
P. O. Box 3473
Peabody, Massachusetts 01961-3473 USA
www.hendricksonrose.com

Book cover by Sergio Urquiza.
Book layout design by Cristalle Kishi.

ISBN: 9781628624489

Printed in the United States of America
010817VP

Contents

Introduction

Today, a man living in the United States has a life expectancy of seventy-eight years. Around the age of forty, he is likely to wonder:

- Who am I?

- Where am I going?

- What am I doing?

- What is the meaning of life?

These questions, and a lot of others, are associated with a man's "midlife." These are serious questions. As a result, our culture often calls a man's asking of them a *crisis*. Thus, the very common phrase, *midlife crisis*.

But it's not just the asking of the questions that makes us refer to this time as a crisis. It is also the way men answer the questions. How a man chooses to experience life's journey determines whether midlife is a crisis or not.

What is the meaning of life?

A cartoon I saw recently portrayed Santa Claus decked out in leather, with the traditional Mrs. Claus telling him he can't trade the old sleigh in for a Harley Davidson no matter how serious of a midlife crisis he is going through.

The joke is, of course, that if Santa traded in the sleigh for a Harley, the world would be in crisis at Christmas—Santa's choice would have huge impact.

The cartoon is worthy of a chuckle. And there is certainly no shortage of jokes and stereotypes circling around midlife, but this book is going to urge you to ignore all the jest and to focus instead on six ways to thrive in midlife. You CAN thrive! You don't have to have a midlife crisis.

This little book will help you answer many questions that accompany midlife. Weighty questions like, "What is my purpose?" can be stepping stones rather than stumbling blocks. Midlife doesn't have to be a crisis of identity or a failure in self-confidence. Midlife can be a season of discovering how your past years and present situation are the very stuff that an exciting future is made of.

You don't have to have a midlife crisis.

I believe with all my heart that

- God has been showing you throughout your life everything you need to thrive in your coming years.

- God, in his infinite wisdom, has been teaching you and preparing you for a great second half.

I encourage you to consider memorizing Psalm 16:11, the theme verse for this book

You make known to me the path of life.

There you have nine, short, simple words that form an amazing truth. Take it to heart. Let it grip you. It's about to take place.

Now let me share with you the following six ways to thrive in midlife. I promise, as you navigate the journey of a man in midlife, you can thrive in these six ways:

1. as Macho Man

2. as a Son

3. as a Husband

4. as a Provider

5. as a Father

6. as a Man of God

Are you ready to THRIVE?

I know you are, but let's look briefly at a crucial prerequisite in the next chapter.

Symptoms of a Crisis

As I prepare this book for publication, the madness of March basketball has begun. One thing I've noticed as I've watched the occasional game is that halftime plays a crucial role if a team wants to win. I've thought for some time now that I could pick the winners if I could just be in the locker rooms at halftime. So, what happens at halftime that enables one team to have a great second half?

I suggest three things take place behind those locker doors:

> **TEACHING:** I think the teams are taught what they need to do in the second half if they're going to carry out a win.

PREPARING: I think, too, that the teams are prepared with the details of how to accomplish what they've been taught—most certainly going over the game plan and making critical adjustments.

ENCOURAGING: I think the teams are encouraged—pumped up and adrenalized—to take the court for the second half and to carry out the demands at hand.

I have watched, probably like you have, two teams go into halftime very close in score—maybe tied, but by the end of the game one team wins by twenty points.

Now of course a tournament game isn't a perfect analogy for your midlife transition, but in the scenario above, the team that is about to get beat by twenty is going through a crisis. And here's the thing: There are signs of that crisis, and they become evident soon into the second half of play. It may be too many turnovers or fouls; lack of defense or hustle; missing open, easy shots; or, most troubling, failure to follow the plan. In other words, a team doesn't get beat for no reason.

Not carrying out a halftime strategy, be it a good plan, a great plan, a poor plan, less of a plan than the other guy, or whatever, is ruinous. To have a plan and not see it through to the best of your ability is a symptom of a crisis unfolding.

SIGNS OF A MIDLIFE CRISIS

So let's say midlife is halftime and you want to thrive in the second half. What's the plan? Have you thought of one? I hope and pray this book provides you with a plan to stick with and refer to often.

Knowing that some men do end up in a crisis should be part of your plan to avoid crisis.

Are you experiencing midlife crisis right now? Is that the reason you picked up this book? Are any of the following resonating with you?

- **DREAMS:** Have you recently remembered some old unfulfilled dreams?

- **REGRETS:** Are you trying to redeem yourself from your regrets?

- **DISILLUSIONMENT:** Are you feeling disillusioned with your life?

- **GUILT:** How about guilt? Are you sensing its crippling effects creeping up on you?

As you read through the six ways to thrive in midlife, keep these four key concepts in mind:

1. **REEVALUATE:** You may have to do some serious reevaluating of your life.

2. **RECALCULATE:** You may have to recalculate critical positions.

3. **REMEMBER:** You may have to remember your past and learn from it.

4. **RE-INSTILL:** You may have to re-instill essential values to properly guide you.

Knowing that there are millions of men in midlife—some stumbling and others thriving—is helpful for all of us men. If you are one of those men in crisis right now, I offer this book as an escape route.

YOU ARE NORMAL AND UNIQUE

Your journey through midlife will be unique to you in most, if not all, ways. For example, you may get a tattoo, but not watch your diet. Your neighbor however, may watch what he eats and get a tattoo and start taking Cialis and comb Rogaine into his hair and buy a Harley.

Midlife is a normal process, though it manifests in unique-to-you ways—if you're fortunate enough to live long enough.

Knowing that some men do end up in a crisis should be part of your plan to avoid crisis.

Gentlemen, this is an important point. Remember, the years of your life are a gift. By now you undoubtedly have friends and colleagues who have passed from this world before they got to experience middle age. Not so with you. You have reached midlife.

CAUTION SIGNS

Just remember, midlife doesn't have to be a crisis. When you treat your midlife years as a gift, you will journey through them a certain way. You will see that dealing with the symptoms of a midlife crisis is a serious matter to take . . . well, to take seriously. Here are the seven symptoms associated with a midlife crisis—they are *the caution signs*.

1. Being Depressed

2. Being Restless

3. Being Irritable

4. Being a "Partier"

5. Being Foolish with Finances

6. Being Obsessed with Sex

7. Being in an Affair

Those are the things to watch for. Let's look at each one in more detail.

1 Being Depressed

I'm not talking about the depression that settles in after your alma mater gets tromped by its top rival on national primetime. I'm talking about the malicious, life-altering, sustained state where you fail to function properly in almost every area of your life. Depression like this is called *clinical depression*, and it's a good idea to get help from a qualified counselor.

Men in midlife suffer from depression because they are convinced that no one appreciates them, and that they aren't doing enough to satisfy the demands placed on them. In a nutshell, these men are convinced they have little value at present.

Are you this man?

- You spend countless hours watching TV or playing video games.

- You eat a lot of junk foods, fast foods, and greasy processed foods.

- You are quick tempered and snarly.

If you are this man, you may be depressed. Keep reading this book.

Do you want to avoid being this man? Keep reading. The six ways to thrive in midlife are coming soon.

2 Being Restless

Are you this man?

- You have very little patience.

- You eat constantly (or so it seems).

- You grumble, grunt, and growl.

- You try one thing, then another, then something else.

- You're getting a tattoo of the Looney Tunes character, Tasmanian Devil on your shoulder.

If you are this man, you may be restless. Keep reading.

Do you want to avoid being this man? Keep reading.

3 Being Irritable

Having patience is a lesson you taught your children. For some reason, men in midlife think they should get a pass on patience. Is that what you think?

Are you this man?

- Do your wife and children ask you, "What's wrong? Why are you so temperamental?"

- You are short-tempered, cross, cantankerous, and touchy.

- People ask you, "What's your problem?" But you're wondering about them, "What's *your* problem, moron?"

If you are this man, you may be irritable. Keep reading.

Do you want to avoid being this man? Keep reading.

4 Being a "Partier"

Are you this man?

- You are suddenly interested in "hanging out with the boys"—spending time in bars and at parties where before you were more of a homebody.

- Your wife and children miss spending time with you and accuse you of neglecting them in favor of being with your friends.

- You have always enjoyed partying, but have taken your partying to new extremes—going out more often or for longer periods of time, drinking more alcohol, and/or experimenting with drugs.

Being a party animal may be a symptom of more than just midlife pleasure-seeking; you may have an addiction. There are real issues at stake, so getting help with this symptom is a good idea.

If you are this man, you may be a partier. Keep reading.

Do you want to avoid being this man? Keep reading.

5 Being Foolish with Finances

Are you this man?

- You are maxing out your credit cards.

- You cashed in your 401K on exotic vacations and red sports cars.

- You are taking on more debt than you should.

Be cautious, gentlemen. Something gets into the mind of some midlife men that makes them think a fancy new sports car is necessary for a happier life. I'm writing from experience here: I had my yellow convertible all decked out.

If you are this man, you may be acting foolishly with your finances. Keep reading.

Do you want to avoid being this man? Keep reading.

6 Being Obsessed with Sex

Are you this man?

- Your fantasies of exotic vacations include exotic women.

- You are using pornography.

- You imagine what it would be like to have a fling with your old high-school or college girlfriend.

Here, I'm referring to engaging the imagination, not engaging in a physical act. However, the next symptom of a midlife crisis is the life-gutting sexual affair. Rarely do men engage in a sexual affair before first indulging their sexual imagination.

If you are this man, you may be obsessed with sex. Keep reading.

Do you want to avoid being this man? Keep reading.

7 Being in an Affair

Are you this man?

- You have engaged in a physically sexual act with a woman other than your wife.

- You have an ongoing sexual relationship with a woman other than your wife.

If you are this man, you may be or have been in an affair. Keep reading.

Do you want to avoid being this man? Keep reading.

The sexual affair is the symptom that should send you to the midlife version of an emergency room for an emergency operation. It is equivalent to the heart attack on the street, which requires ambulance assistance and a multiple-bypass operation.

If you are pursuing a sexual affair, you are about to make a country song of your life.

But are you without hope? Absolutely not! Start praying for mercy, grace, and understanding from everyone you're hurting—none of which you deserve.

And take the following steps:

- Call the other woman, and tell her you are breaking it off. Again, *call* her; do not see her in person.

- Apologize for your shortsightedness and ask her to forgive you.

- Make sure she knows it is over; that she should never expect from you a call, email, or text; and that you will not respond to any attempted communication from her.

- Change your phone numbers and email addresses.

- Block her on your social media accounts.

- Call 1–800–NEW–LIFE, and get connected with a counselor in your area.

- Join a support group like Celebrate Recovery.

- Confess to your wife when your counselor tells you to do so.

- Optional: Email me at SArterburn@newlife.com

You should take the seven above symptoms seriously. Do not let your midlife be lessened by giving in to them. In fact, you should adjust your thinking right now and think of your middle years as the best years of your life.

LET US ADMIT SOME THINGS

You are probably not dealing with all seven symptoms of a midlife crisis. Struggling through one or two, or even three of them is possible. But rare is it to be a man deep in depression, clamoring after every new gadget, partying four nights a week, dropping thousands of dollars on merchandise, and hustling after a cheap affair.

Think of your middle years as the best years of your life.

However, let us admit that:

- We are carrying more weight on our bodies than ten years ago—and in weirder places.

- We have less hair than five years ago.

- We feel less strength in our bones than we did last year.

- We think we're less connected to others than we were yesteryear.

- We are watching more TV and missing some things from our former lifestyle.

And let's admit that a lot of the above apparently crept up on us like a mugger. That, my fellow men, is the scary thing about midlife. It happens all of a sudden, or so it seems.

And it does no good to deny the symptoms.

MUGGED BY MORTALITY

It's your fortieth birthday and you look in the mirror. Who is that standing behind you? He's there every morning. In fact, he's there every time you look in a mirror. It's your mortality and now that you're thinking about him again, you're pretty certain he's lurking in the shadow of every step you take.

The realization of your own mortality arrives when you stop believing you are young and immortal. It arrives with midlife.

- Maybe it arrived when you tore ligaments in your knee playing a pick-up game—you've played a thousand games and all of a sudden, you're sidelined with a blown-out knee.

- Maybe it arrived when you got a hernia at work. But you've always been able to lift 150 pounds, no problem. Not anymore.

You've been mugged by mortality. The blown-out knee and the hernia only foreshadow what is coming. You are not immortal.

This realization arrives sooner or later and when it does, one significant thing happens: You begin to think long and hard about

- The kind of person you have been

- The kind of person you are

- The kind of person you want to be—i.e., how you want to be remembered when mortality is complete

Most men answer honestly that they want to be a man of quality and character, or something like that. I've never met a man who wanted to be a perpetual jerk for all his remaining years.

A lot of men say they want to honor God with their life; they want to be faithful and pleasing to the Lord. As a fellow Christian, I applaud this sentiment. And that is why the following six ways to thrive in midlife incorporate ways to honor God.

> *A lot of men say they want to honor God with their life.*

THE ROLES YOU PLAY

 ### Taking a Look Back

The reason I have six ways to thrive is because, as men, we have distinct roles to play in life. We are sons, husbands, providers, and fathers. And you're thinking right now, "Hmmm, that is four, not six." Of course, you're correct.

In those four roles, you will thrive throughout midlife if you keep reading and adopt for yourself the plan I've laid out. The other two ways are bookends to the big four. They hold you together by bringing clarity to your life. You'll see what I mean shortly.

Lacking a Role or Two

But what if you don't play all four roles? Perhaps you're not a father or a husband. Well, I'd suggest you read them anyway. You never know what you might glean from them, or when they might very much apply to your life.

Changing Roles

It is also helpful to remember how your roles have changed.

- You've been a good son for forty years, but now your parents need you to care for them in new ways.

- You've been a good, steady provider for all of your career, but now you're finding that aspects of your career have changed drastically, and you need to go back to school or face becoming obsolete.

- You've been "World's #1 Dad" to your children, but your children are now adults with children of their own. Now you're granddad.

The big take away is times have changed and you've changed over time.

Here's how I summarize the reality you're facing:

> So here we are, in life that's clearly become a production radically different from the one in which we're used to starring. Suddenly, it seems as if everybody's character in the show has changed and nobody's sticking to the script; the action's not like anything we've rehearsed before. Pieces of the set are getting dragged off into the wings, lights are blinking all over the place—all kinds of things are going on that we've never even almost experienced.[1]

Would you go see this show? I think you would. I think you should. It has everything required to be a blockbuster.

And best of all: God wrote the script! He has brought you through every year up

It is also helpful to remember how your roles have changed.

to this point, and he intends to see you through midlife and lead you toward the life he desires for you to have.

LET'S GET INTO IT

For the six ways to thrive in midlife:

- ■ First, I'll pinpoint things that can thwart thriving.

- ■ I will follow that up by spotlighting things that can inspire thriving.

- ■ Then it's time to pull out one big takeaway from each role.

Everything is up for you to take or leave, but my sole intent is for you to benefit.

Macho Man

I use the term *Macho Man* to explain who we are as men. Macho Man enlightens us to ourselves, so we should recognize a lot of our thoughts, actions, and desires in him.

MACHO MAN: THINGS THAT THWART THRIVING

Hard as it is to admit, the following four ideas about being a man are in every man's DNA. And they can be real hindrances during midlife.

1 God's Gift to Everyone

Do you know this man?

- He has the answers for everything.
-

- He is never wrong.

- He catches the biggest fish.

- He grills the best barbeque.

- He runs the show at home (according to what he tells the boys at work).

- He runs the show at work (according to what he tells everyone else).

He has one thing correct: He's a show. He's not real. He can't let himself be real, there's too much poser in him. In short, this is his self-obsessed gene.

However, before you get too critical, check the list below and determine how many of the statements you agree with. What do you believe it means to be a man?

BEING A MAN MEANS:	YES	NO
Knowing everything		
Being a woman magnet		
Being in total control of my emotions		

BEING A MAN MEANS:	YES	NO
Making sure it is obvious that I make a ton of money		
Making sure it is obvious that I am exceptionally wise		
Being naturally athletic		
Having *all* my plans work out perfectly *always*		
Never being hurt in any way		
Being gifted mechanically		

Let's be honest—this concept of Macho Man is in every man, to one degree or another.

But is it really possible to be *that* strong? Can you really be *that* brilliant? Probably not; you would be on the level of Superman. (By the way, Superman isn't real!)

What do you believe it means to be a man?

2 Entitled to Rule and Reign

Macho Man may not say it verbatim, but he's thinking that he is entitled to rule and reign. How about you?

- Do you think you should have special rights?

- Are you endowed by your Creator to have special privileges?

- How about benefits at work? Shouldn't you be allowed extra-long breaks because you work so hard?

Entitlement boils down to three things:

- Wanting as much control as you can get

- Having power over as many people as possible

- Expecting special privileges just because you are you

Have you seen where entitlement commonly shows up? At home, that's where—with the people who love you the most. Millions of men march around their home like it's their personal kingdom to reign.

For some reason, men act at home in a way they'd never act anywhere else. At home, they feel like they have the right to mumble and grumble and fly off the handle and be impossibly impatient or rudely dismissive.

And what does God think? I'm not sure we want to know what God thinks of our arrogance and acts of entitlement.

3 Never Express Emotions

Just don't ever express emotion and you'll never have to show you're anything but a Macho Man— or James Bond, or a typical rock 'em, sock 'em movie hero.

Men are subtly—and not so subtly—taught that "real" men don't show emotions. How does this happen to us? I think we learned it from our dads, who learned it from their dads. We are supposed to be strong, and of course, in the definition of strong, there is no reference to revealing emotions.

Never express emotions and no one will ever know you have a heart. We are told that revealing your heart, especially to other men, is foolhardy. But if you never express emotions, you're more likely to be an emotional basket case in midlife.

4 Handle the Tough Stuff Alone

If you are faced with a tough situation that involves you getting emotional, it is best to handle it alone. That is another way we Macho Men are wired or trained.

Men are subtly—and not so subtly— taught that "real" men don't show emotions.

It is assumed *real* men will carry the heavy burdens in life on their back all alone—up hill and in the snow.

One of the unwritten rules of manhood is not to burden another person—especially another man—with any weighty matter. You may check out a library book to look for answers, but don't tell anyone you went to the library.

Like them or not, these four ideas are fundamental to who we are as men. It takes discipline to keep them in check. It takes a daily dose of knowing who we are in Christ—a sinner saved by grace once we've put our faith in Him.

MACHO MAN: THINGS THAT INSPIRE THRIVING

1 Power to Achieve

It is absolutely true of men that they possess power to achieve many things. This isn't just about running a marathon or winning a golf tournament, though those things are within a man's power to achieve. Macho Man is also empowered to solve emergencies around his home:

- Garbage disposal breaks down

- Car needs oil

- A burglar comes around (Heaven forbid!)

Men have the ability to "step up" in crunch time.

Men have the ability to "step up" in crunch time.

The movies we saw as boys helped instill this in us. For example, we saw firemen putting out fires, and soldiers winning at war.

Above all, instead of being egotistical about this power, Macho Man understands that power is a gift from God to accomplish what God wants to accomplish.

2 Responsibility

Another inspiring aspect of being a man—or Macho Man—is understanding your responsibilities and actually being content to carry them out in your daily life.

You are being responsible if you:

- Pay your bills

- Have an up-to-date will

- Mow your lawn

- Take care of the trash

▪ Change light bulbs and furnace filters

Responsibility means work, and by midlife you should understand the importance of the work you need to do. Macho Man has learned the value in being a real man with responsibilities. Over the years of a man's life, he learns through sometimes painful consequences why neglecting responsibilities doesn't work. He learns that being irresponsible and not doing the tough things when they need to be done leads to worse situations and bigger mountains to climb.

3 Mountain Moving

Speaking of mountains, when a man decides to roll up his sleeves, stand back! He's going to move a mountain and get some work done.

One of the finest desirable aspects of being a Macho Man is coming to the realization that staying on task, sticking to the work at hand, going about something in little by little stages, will eventually prove rewarding.

IT IS ABOUT HAVING PATIENCE.

Yes, patience is a virtue!

On the contrary, giving up quickly, not seeing something through to its end, jumping from one thing to the next with little thought of accomplishment, is evidence that Macho Man is still rather immature. Buckling down to move the many mountains you face is evidence of maturity. Trying for a shortcut is immature; it is what children do. There are some things in a man's life that will require work—long, hard hours of sweaty work.

4 Bravery

When you've conquered several of those mountains, you no longer fear what may be coming. You've learned:

- Patience
- Persistence
- Perspective

Simply stated, you've learned another inspiring feature of the Macho Man: bravery.

Here's the deal, early in your life you feared many things. But you had parents and others around to help handle your fears. Oftentimes, as a grown man, you face fears alone, or with your wife who needs your strength, and it is never easy. But after you conquer a few of them, you grow in confidence that you'll be able to overcome other troubling fears.

By midlife, you have overcome many things and you have a legitimate claim to bravery. You are rightly positioned to overcome any fears about midlife. Remember, overcoming past fears has made you brave in the face of any coming situation you may fear.

By midlife, you have overcome many things and you have a legitimate claim to bravery.

Of course, there will be something that arises and makes your heart stop a moment. There will always be things that intimidate us, if we're honest. But then you get the right perspective of the thing and face it head on with every intention of overcoming it.

This is your claim to bravery.

OUR LESSON FROM BEING MACHO MAN

What's the big takeaway about being a Macho Man? **INTEGRITY.** You will thrive in midlife and beyond if your masculinity is pursued with integrity. In other words, go ahead and be Macho Man, but be Macho Man with integrity.

But what is integrity? The American Heritage Dictionary defines integrity as "Steadfast adherence to a strict moral or ethical code."

It fits. It is integrity that will separate the Macho Men who merely know what morals and ethics are, from the Macho Men who will steadfastly adhere to their morals and ethical code.

THE GRAY AREAS

As a man embracing his middle years, you have learned that life is not black and white, but that there are a lot of gray areas. You've learned:

- To wait, watch, and listen to discern something, or someone, or a situation

- To stand back from a scene and appraise it, and then take steps for a closer, possibly clearer appraisal

- How to be responsible

- How to handle the tough stuff in life

- How to be brave

You've become strong and wise.

Over the years, you've acquired all of these qualities and more. They have fashioned a strict moral and ethical code that has you swearing off the foolish things of the world and glomming onto what has value:

- Your relationship with God

- Your discernment between right and wrong

- Your love for family and friends

- Your commitments and promises

The bottom line is your masculinity—your Macho Man masculinity—has integrity. With it you will thrive in midlife.

2

Son

The first and one of the primary roles you fill during your lifetime is that of being a son. For one reason or another, son is a relationship you may deny or possibly ignore, but you can never be entirely free of it. You were born the son of someone and the truth of it shows up in the mirror every day.

Most likely, you have embraced your sonship. More than likely, you have wrestled through the years to figure out exactly what it means to be a son. You may have a pretty good grasp on it by now. Then again, the role of son changes readily, so maybe you're facing another change.

In the age we live, we have divorce, multiple marriages, fatherlessness, and single parenting confusing the issue. Being a son is not as easily defined as it was during biblical times when a long and coveted genealogy was kept. Back then, I surmise, a son knew exactly to whom he belonged and what was expected of him for each and every season of his life.

I think God recorded genealogies because being a son is truly significant.

Today, it is certainly more complicated.

Here is an insightful bit on the biblical sons of Asher: "The sons of Asher . . . were . . . heads of families, choice men, brave warriors and outstanding leaders"(1 Chronicles 7:30,40).

How cool would it be to know this about your ancestors? If you were somewhere down the line in the genealogy of Asher, don't you think you would be emboldened to live life with passion? I mean, shoot, it looks to me like the sons of Asher thrived!

Understanding the Family Tree

If you read the Bible and come to a section of

genealogy you probably skim it or skip it. But even those of us who find other people's genealogies boring, are interested in our own genealogies.

- What do you know about your genealogy?

- Has what you know equipped you for life?

- Has it helped you thrive?

- Are there things that you have intentionally rejected because they would hamper your health—such as a family history of drug or alcohol abuse?

Answering yes to any of these questions is a sign that you are concerned about your genealogy.

God has included genealogies in his Word and has preserved them for thousands of years, so they must have their benefits. I think God recorded genealogies because being a son is truly significant.

Catch that? Being a son is truly significant.

Truly Significant

Being a son is truly significant to who Jesus is. Two of the gospels include the genealogy of Jesus.

- "This is the genealogy of Jesus the Messiah the son of David, the son of Abraham . . . and Jacob the father of Joseph, the husband of Mary, and Mary was the mother of Jesus who is called the Messiah" (Matthew 1:1,16).

- "Now Jesus himself was about thirty years old when he began his ministry. He was the son, so it was thought, of Joseph. . . the son of God" (Luke 3:23,38).

From them we learn that:

- Jesus is divine and human.

- He is God's own eternal son.

- He was born of a woman.

Christians believe Jesus Christ is the "God-man," which is one theological word you may have seen or heard, which tries to express the truth that Jesus is fully God and fully human.

How about the role of sonship that you have?

- Do you believe that being a son is significant to your life?

- What has the relationship looked like for you over the years leading up to midlife?

- How do you think the relationship will look in the future?

I think by the end of this chapter, you'll see how significant being a son truly is. Remember Psalm 16:11, our verse from earlier:

You make known to me the path of life.

SON: THINGS THAT THWART THRIVING

1 Physical Dependence

Let's start where we all began, as infants—helpless, entirely dependent babies. That's right, you cannot deny that at one time in your life you needed someone. If you've had children of your own, you are even more aware of just how incredibly helpless you were as a baby.

You would have never grown without someone attending to your physical needs. You were unable to eat or drink without help.

And the big hurt about being physically dependent is, you had no say in anything. If you were put in an outfit that matched your sister's, then it was just too bad if you didn't like it. If you were having peas and carrots, then that is what you were having. Yep, no say whatsoever in anything.

You cannot deny that at one time in your life you needed someone.

Here's the killer question about physical dependence that will thwart you thriving in midlife: You were a helpless baby; are you now a helpless man?

Ouch! But it may be true. Countless men arrive at midlife still physically dependent on parents in some way. Of course, it's not the eating and diapers anymore, but how about a loan of money or looking for a place to stay?

This dependence doesn't bode well when as a son, you have to start taking responsibility for your parents. It sometimes happens suddenly and other times gradually; but the time *will* come when your parents—the people you were and maybe still are dependent on—will need you to care for them physically and maybe even financially. It is better that you are preparing for this eventuality rather than making your parents think and feel like you will always be dependent on them.

2 Emotional Dependence

Pick an emotion and ask how your parents came to feel it.

- Did your parents get upset at certain things?

- What made your parents happy?

- What frustrated them?

How about you? Do you find that the very things that upset, angered, frustrated, made happy, or scared your parents are the very things that turn your emotions the same way?

LIKE FATHER, LIKE SON.

Maybe you are not so independent after all. Maybe you've separated from your parents physically, but emotionally you act exactly as your parents did when you were growing up. That's emotional dependence and it is common. It will thwart your thriving if you don't identify the unhealthy aspects and work to ditch them.

3 Immature Thinking

Juveniles aren't taken very seriously. Even if, as an adolescent, you were brilliant and stood on grand principles, there were plenty of adults who discredited your ideas as childish and fleeting. Some people never outgrow being discredited that way. They continue to think everyone will judge their ideas as immature and adolescent.

If you assume you are still adolescent in your thinking, you're going to have a hard time thriving in midlife.

- Know that your knowledge has matured as you have.

- Remind yourself that you don't think like a child anymore.

If someone says you think childishly, find out what he or she meant. Then, deal with it if it is valid, or shrug it off if it is not. You don't want to be a man who, in his thinking, is still in middle school instead of midlife.

4 Believing in Your Parents' Wrong Beliefs

You have surely absorbed a few of your parents' beliefs. It is quite natural to do so. As mentioned above, we had no control over our childhoods.

- We did what our parents wanted.

- We listened to what they listened to.

- We went to the places they went.

- We thought as they did and felt as they felt.

- We learned from them everything we were going to know.

At least we did for many years, so it is entirely understandable that we would develop our beliefs around those of our parents.

But this could be a problem if your parents were just plain wrong about something. To determine if one of your beliefs is misguided because you got it from your parents:

- Find out if it really is a wrong belief.

- Isolate it from that which is true.

- Remove it entirely along with its roots.

It is a mature decision to examine your beliefs to see if they are balanced and true. The Bereans, Paul tells us, "received the message with great eagerness and examined the Scriptures every day to see if what Paul said was true" (Acts 17:11). You and I would do well to do the same, even if a belief comes to us from our most trusted confidante.

You'll thrive in midlife when you discover a belief you learned from you parents needs to be released and you get to the business of doing so. If you don't— if you cling out of sentimentality or any other reason to a wrong belief—this thing will thwart your thriving.

You can't change who your parents are. You received who the good Lord gave you. And that was for a reason. And you may think there is no escaping who you are because of who your father was—and people have always said you're just like your father. Be it anger or apathy or any other trait or wrong message you believed about yourself, the fact is that you can change.

Breathe a sigh of relief that you can change your future by letting go of your past.

The key now is to identify wrong beliefs and messages and be healed from them. You don't have to fear anything from your past and you don't have to resent anyone from your past. What you should do is breathe a sigh of relief that you can change your future by letting go of your past.

Let's look at the things that inspire thriving in the role of son. It really comes down to maximizing the best attributes you have as a son.

SON: THINGS THAT INSPIRE THRIVING

1 The Thrilling Joys of Boyhood

You probably have some vivid memories of being
a boy and the fun you had being free to play—just
play and play and play.

- Was it a sandlot?

- Was it a woodlot?

- Was it a parking lot?

Where were your freest moments spent? I bet you
can remember because the joys experienced in that
place got stamped on your heart forever.

And you know what? In the hectic pace of midlife,
you should recall boyhood joys and relish the
moments of that bygone era. There is no reason
to bury such pleasures just because you are now
a *grown-up*.

2 The Golden Lessons of Boyhood

Can you list one or two things you learned about
life when you were just a boy? I'm talking about

the one or two timeless lessons you learned when you were the apple of your mother's eye and the joy of your father.

You can probably list several. Maybe some of the lessons below are on your list:

- Don't kick or hit a girl.

- Respect your teachers.

- Honor your parents.

- Play by the rules.

- Do your chores.

- Hold the door for your mom and sister.

- Be honest.

- Listen when being spoken to.

- Speak when called upon.

These are just a few. A lot of men know these golden lessons by heart because they were trained as sons to practice them.

Our society will be worse off if we fail to pass these golden lessons on to our sons. And not when they're in high school or college, but when they are young, impressionable boys.

3 Surviving Life's Early Licks

This has more to do with being a son of society, than your parents' son. To one degree or another, the society in which you grew up had an influence in "raising" you. Every son of society has taken his share of licks. You just can't grow up without them. And this truth bodes well for thriving in midlife adventures.

Suppose you get fired because your position was outsourced or your company is downsizing. So what? This isn't a big deal compared to how you were mocked, ignored, and excluded from stuff all through boyhood. These are specific examples that may not apply to you, but the lesson here is that emotionally, you've "been there, done that." You've

Our society will be worse off if we fail to pass these golden lessons on to our sons when they are young, impressionable boys.

learned how to survive the tough emotional stuff. Now in midlife and later on in life, you can keep emotional challenges in perspective because of what you've already survived.

You survived licks as a boy, as a young man, and up through the years; so there is no reason you won't keep taking licks and keep surviving them.

4 Affection for Family

You're older now, and more and more folks will be telling you so. What else will they be telling you? Very likely, many will tell you how much you resemble your father. Do you know what it is they are talking about? They mean your personality and possibly your appearance resembles your father's.

Is it true? Yep!

You see, something magical happens in midlife: You are no longer ashamed of resembling your father. When you were younger you may have cringed when anyone said you looked or acted like your dad. *What?* You didn't want to be that old man!

Now you are older and you have actually reflected a little more about the qualities of your father, and

lo and behold, you kind of
desire the same for yourself.

Of course, this isn't the case
for every man going into
midlife. Some men will never
appreciate their fathers; and
sometimes their reasons are
well founded. They want
to change the legacy, not
promote a bad one.

*Thriving involves
being a man
with substance;
it involves being
a man who
cares less about
appearance
and more about
deep-seated
matters.*

But many millions of men
grow to appreciate their
family—father, mother, and
siblings, too. For them—and hopefully, for you—
the affection infects their purposes for the future.
It not only infects, but it injects a reason to thrive
into their life's purposes.

What you discover sometime around midlife is the
depths to which you were affected by your family
in positive ways. And now that glowing legacy is
something you want to pass on to your children
and grandchildren. Thriving involves being a man
with substance; it involves being a man who cares
less about appearance and more about deep-seated

matters. And believe it or not there is real freedom in this.

OUR LESSON FROM BEING A SON

So how do we bring this role of being a son to a nice resolution? What is the big takeaway? It is **ADVENTURE**.

You will thrive in midlife and beyond if you would pursue life the way a boy who is free to play pursues life. Remember that free-to-play life? There was so much spontaneous adventure growing up. You just went about being who you were and you did it how boys do it. There was no care for "who we should be" or "how we should be."

Where did that carefree adventuring go? How did we get so far from adventuring?

Here is the answer:

- The wandering cowboy took ownership of the ranch.

- The knight in shining armor married a princess.

- The intrepid explorer settled into a career, built a home, and had a family.

In other words, as you were becoming a man, you almost unnoticeably took on the demands of being a man.

- You became more serious.

- You put in more effort.

- You became determined.

- You got tough.

- You hit the grind.

In a nutshell, you stopped being a boy and became a man. And there is nothing wrong with that. Actually, like we discovered earlier, if you didn't take on the demands of manhood there is something wrong.

But it is time to recapture some of the boyhood adventuring. I'm talking about recapturing the underlying source of adventure. I don't mean leaving the house half painted, walking into the woods, finding a stick for a horse, and riding off over the hill to wrangle cattle. I don't mean getting your son's little green army men and pretending you're in the battle of the century. This isn't about that kind of pretending.

And I don't suggest you become irresponsible. You still remain serious-minded about serious matters. Let reality be reality, but see what is going on in the life of a son who is free to play and then model that.

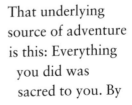

That underlying source of adventure is this: Everything you did was sacred to you. By sacred I mean your heart, soul, mind, and strength enveloped what you pursued—and it did this naturally, without pretense.

- Everything was truly important to you

- Everything had special significance

- Everything was really treasured

- Everything was totally trusted

- Everything was worthy of your complete devotion

- Everything held your utmost attention

Middle age is the time to recapture sacredness.

Every time you went out to the sandlot, a new adventure came your way and you devoted your boyhood self to it. Every time you walked into the woods was as important as the last. Whatever you did, you committed your time, energy, and will to it.

Middle age is the time to recapture sacredness. This is the big takeaway from being a son.

- If having to care for parents who cared for you stresses you out, think of it as an adventure—a sacred one.

- If your career is at a dead end, put your heart, soul, mind, and strength back into it in new unique ways—as if you were showing up for your first day every day.

Apply this adventuring to every midlife situation.

Remember, you became a man in order to survive the world that came around you. You did what was right: The world demanded you mature, and so you matured.

But now you are a man, an approved man, and now you're in midlife. So bring back the unabashed, boyhood adventure, bring back sacredness. And, gentlemen, you will thrive.

— **3** —

Husband

Another primary role you fill during your lifetime is that of being a husband. Now wait a minute, I'm a smart, professional guy so there is no way I think that I'm only writing to married men. Plus, there's an editor on this and lots of smart people that wouldn't let me get away with such a thing. Many of you reading this right now are not married. See, I told you—I'm a pro.

Seriously though, there are many reasons you may be single.

- Maybe you are divorced.

- Maybe you will be married at some point in the future.

- Maybe you are a widower.

- Maybe you have had multiple marriages.

- Maybe you were engaged, with the date set, tickets purchased for the honeymoon, and then the whole thing got called off.

If you are currently single, know there is nothing wrong with singleness and read this part anyway. Perhaps you were previously married, and your life and your sense of yourself have been affected by fulfilling the role of husband. Plus, you may find a beautiful woman to marry and you should be ready for that reality.

Will you love her, comfort her, honor and keep her, in sickness and in health, and forsaking every other, keep to her only, so long as you both shall live?

Here is that reality:

- You see a woman you want to meet

- Or you are introduced to a woman

- You have a date or two or three or more

- You become a couple

- You kiss (the kissing may come earlier)

- You propose marriage

And then, before God, family, and friends . . . comes the solemnization of marriage. The minister says something like, "Let us pray. Dearly beloved, we are assembled here in the sight of God and in the presence of this company to join this man and this woman in the bonds of holy marriage . . ."

Dearly beloved, hear what the Apostle Paul says: "Wives, submit yourselves to your own husbands as you do to the Lord. . . . as the church submits to Christ. . . . Husbands, love your wives, just as Christ loved the church and gave himself up for her." (Ephesians 5:22,24–25).

Husbands, love your wives? Yep!

After that, we have the vows:

> Do you take [name of woman here], before God
> and these witnesses, to be your wedded wife? Will
> you love her, comfort her, honor and keep her, in
> sickness and in health, and forsaking every other,
> keep to her only, so long as you both shall live?

Gentlemen, there you have reality as parsed as
I can make it without bordering on disrespect.
Because I believe from the formation of a
relationship respect should be elevated.

- Would you say, "I do"?

- If you are married, did you say, "I do"?

And then what? Well, you live happily ever after.
Right?

But like being a son is more complicated than
all the surface stuff, so is being a husband more
complicated than the vows suggest it should be.

It is also true that being married for five, ten,
fifteen, twenty, or thirty years changes the role
of husband. How would you say your role of
husband has changed? How has your life changed?

- Having children

- Seeing your children leave the home

- Caring for elderly parents

- Dealing with career challenges

- Watching your body change

- Watching your wife's body change

All of these realities impact your role as husband.

HUSBAND: THINGS THAT THWART THRIVING

1 Fixated with Sex

Do you still think about sex the way you did when you were nineteen or twenty? You may have to readjust your thinking when you take on the middle years as a married man.

- Husband #1 is insane about sex the way he was in college. He thinks all physical contact should lead to orgasm. However, his wife would rather be held and loved and readied to respond to him in sexual ways.

- Husband #2 is more than willing to hold his wife, lie with her, talk, listen, and ultimately make love, leading to her satisfaction. He understands the role of being her husband, not her being his conquest.

It is your choice. It really is. With the prescription and over-the-counter drugs now available for men to have the kind of sexual prowess they had in their twenties, it is possible to still act as immaturely as you did then.

Instead, take your cues from God's Word:

- "May your fountain be blessed, and may you rejoice in the wife of your youth. A loving doe, a graceful deer—may her breasts satisfy you always, may you ever be intoxicated with her love" (Proverbs 5:18–19).

■ "Enjoy life with your wife, whom you love. … For this is your lot in life" (Ecclesiastes 9:9).

Pick those passages apart, meditate on them daily, and pretty soon you'll see in them a portrait of a husband thriving sexually in midlife. Words like rejoice, love, graceful, satisfy, always, and enjoy concoct a beautiful image of long and satisfying love.

2 Living the Old Lies

Men get the idea that we have to show our neighbor (if not the whole world) that we are a certain kind of man. By the time we get to midlife, we've pretty much perfected the lies we tell others—and ourselves—that portray the image we want to convey.

This pattern of lying begins when we are young men and continues . . . well, it continues until we decide to stop living the same old lies. As young men, we didn't know ourselves or even *how* to know ourselves. We didn't really know how to learn about the world around us, and so we began to fake and fudge things in an effort to discover answers. It's a trial-and-error process until we've found out what works for us, and what humiliates or defeats us.

Where are you at on this?
Are you still concerned with your image?
On the spectrum of style versus substance,
where would you put your mark?

Along the way, we get fairly caught-up in portraying the image that works, so we stick to it, and build on it when we need to.

One of the biggest problems, however, is that the image we are lying about goes into our marriage with us. It takes reaching midlife before we want to shed the old lies, in the same way a slithering snake sheds old skin.

If you do shed the old lies you're better off than those who don't. If you don't lose the image the lies will thwart thriving.

Midlife can be especially fruitful when you finally realize that you know yourself better than you thought. This can have an immediate influence on being a husband:

- You become more honest with your wife about your fears and insecurities.

- You tell her all about what you've learned about yourself.

- And, of greatest importance, you let her help you understand more than before.

Why is this so important to being a husband? Because now your wife has the husband God created him to be. And she is his helper. This is fulfilling her God-ordained purpose in marriage. As a result, she feels closer than ever to you. Most likely, you are her best and dearest friend. And most likely, you will truly share together in the grace of life.

3 Keep Taking Your Wife for Granted

"But I don't take my wife for granted," you may say. Okay, let me put it this way: When was the last time your wife told you that she felt you appreciated her ultimate value in the marriage?

Now you're probably thinking, "You better watch it, Steve. You're hitting awfully close to home."

And don't I know it all too well.

The Bible tells us, "Everyone should be quick to listen, slow to speak and slow to become angry" (James 1:19). As men, we don't do *any* of these well—especially with our wives. Sheesh. What's wrong with us? This is the woman who loves us best, and what do we do?

- We dismiss her.

- We ignore her.

- We become impatient with her.

- We get angry and short-tempered with her.

There is no end to our taking her for granted.

An old adage says, "Time changes everything." Ask an older man what this means and he'll likely tell you that:

- He is now less inclined to impose his will on others.

- He respects others more.

- He is more reflective before making important decisions.

- Overall, he is more objective in life.

If this older man does answer this way, ask him to mentor you! If he doesn't, then he is the one who needs a mentor.

Midlife is the time these changes in perspective begin to take place. One impetus for change is the realization that we don't know our wives nearly as well as we ought.

How do you spend your daily allowance of time?

Thus, midlife is a great time to begin renewal and rediscovery of your wife. Keep taking her for granted and struggle indefinitely with thriving. But treat her daily like the precious treasure she is and you'll thrive as a husband.

HUSBAND: THINGS THAT INSPIRE THRIVING

1 Invaluable Time

Time is one of the great mysteries, universally recognized as an enigma. You may keep it with a watch or on the wall, but you really are not keeping time. Time cannot be kept; time only passes. And as far as a day is concerned, we all have the same amount of time to pass.

How do you spend your daily allowance of time?

Of course, much of your time has been wasted, for none of us is perfect. But one place you've spent a significant amount of time is on relationships. One of those is your wife. And this proves to be invaluable time as you traverse midlife. Time spent with your wife has taught you the finer qualities for good living—in fact they are criterion for thriving.

- Love
- Sacrifice
- Humility
- Patience
- Acceptance
- Kindness
- Faithfulness
- Gentleness
- Self-control

If these look familiar, it is because the Bible calls them the *fruit of the Spirit*. "The fruit of the Spirit is love, joy, peace, forbearance, kindness, goodness, faithfulness, gentleness and self-control" (Galatians 5:22–23).

And so, it is good for a husband to ask himself how he wants to spend his time going into the future. You and I know that during the course of our lives we have allowed certain things to consume more time than they deserve (i.e., watching television). Thankfully the invaluable time you've spent with your wife, though not a perfect amount, has set you up for thriving.

2 Compromise

What needs to be said about compromise? It depends. Here are the options:

- First, you get it. You would not still be married and reading this if you didn't understand the true value of compromise.

- Second, if you haven't understood the true value of compromise yet, all it means is your ego-driven, self-centered, take-care-of-number-one attitude still reigns.

By nature, we are sinful. We are selfish, self-centered, self-consumed, and basically concerned only about ourselves. Compromise is thus contrary to your ego-driven self. What you should do is consider your real purpose in life: What is the highest aim of man?

The answer is to love God and to bring glory to him forever. Your self-centeredness doesn't do that. And so it is time to readjust some things.

Submitting your will to God's will is the most important kind of compromising.

As a husband who wants to thrive:

> Compromise is the ability and willingness to make your own will and your own needs subservient to love. God know our needs. What we need more than anything is an everyday, readily comprehended, love-based means of understanding that life is all about learning to give up our personal will for his divine love.[2]

3 Heroism

Submitting your will to God's will is the most important kind of compromising.

Heroism inspires thriving. How? Your wife thinks of you as a hero. Not a sports hero or a superhero, but the hero who shovels the snow, and empties trash, and rushes somewhere to pick up something needed in an emergency.

Your wife also responds to her hero. You can't remember your own heroism, but she does. She has certain heroic deeds locked away in her memory forever.

Just stay the course and thriving, as your wife's hero/husband, won't be a problem.

4 God Is on Your Side

This is real inspiration for men approaching or living the middle years. Even more importantly, it is *true*. Since the time you put faith in Jesus to forgive your sins, you have had the help of the Holy Spirit with you:

- "Jesus answered, 'I am the way and the truth and the life. No one comes to the Father except through me'" (John 14:6).

- "I will ask the Father, and he will give you another advocate to help you and be with you forever—the Spirit of truth. The world cannot accept him, because it neither sees him nor knows him. But you know him, for he lives with you and will be in you" (John 14:16–17).

You are able to look back over your life and see your Lord God leading you.

As middle-aged men, you have witnessed firsthand the complexity of married life. You have also witnessed many of those complexities smooth out. You have witnessed, while holding the hand of your wife, seemingly insurmountable obstacles be scaled.

You are able to look back over your life and see your Lord God leading you. He has abided with you. He has been your God. He has revealed himself to you in the everyday—and often mundane—stuff you and your wife have gone through together.

And you know what? God promises he will never leave you nor forsake you (Deuteronomy 31:6). Straight ahead is your course through your middle years, and God is on your side. I know I believe, as a married man in midlife, it is empowering to know God is on my side.

It is also exciting!

OUR LESSON FROM BEING A HUSBAND

What is the big takeaway from this role of husband? It is **LOVE**.

Does your wife know absolutely everything about you? We men have a long history of keeping secrets and other things to ourselves. Of course, we believe God knows everything about us; there is no keeping anything from our all-knowing God. But how about our life partner here in this world?

- Does your wife know your dreams?

- Does she know about your fears?

- Does she know what you'd like to pursue or achieve or risk?

- Do you keep any secret hobbies or habits from her?

- Do you use any covers—like staying late at the office, not to do office work but to actually work on a book you've always wanted to write?

Come on, gentlemen, let us do better. Doing any of these hurts our chances of thriving. Our wives should be our friends; stop pretending to be what you're not. Start telling them everything, even if it carries momentary discomfort.

What does all this have to do with being a husband who is loving? The answer is that you are not young anymore! And, newsflash, you are not getting any younger! You only have so much time left to love your wife for who she is, and to be loved by your wife for exactly who you are.

Give up your protective cover. Show your scars and cracks. Would you? You will be her best friend and she will be yours. Then, like lovers and friends do—and like husbands and wives should—you will have a lot of loving fun together.

Provider

What do you do for work?

This is the most popular question at the society clubs of New York. It is the most common inquiry in the social halls of a church. The import of the question is, of course, to find out what a person does. It is a defining question. It is sometimes a welcome question and sometimes it scares guys.

But for all it is, it makes complete sense in our age to ask what a man does. What a man does for work carries a lot of weight for him.

"What you do for work?" is the most asked question among men.

Right or wrong:

- A man's identity often correlates directly to his work.

- A man's security is felt deeply and derives from his work.

- A man's self-worth comes in a big way from his work.

And so enters into this little book the role of Provider, a.k.a., Breadwinner or Bringer-home-of-the-bacon.

PROVIDER: THINGS THAT THWART THRIVING

1 Being Defined by Your Position and Title

You can handle this for a time. You can handle it for many years in fact. But when midlife comes around, you want to see yourself and be seen by others with a deeper significance. Letting your position and title define you may very well stymie the idea that you can thrive in midlife. The idea going into midlife is to lessen the pressures

Providing for our family is something we men take very seriously. It has to be a strand in our DNA—and not a short, thin strand either, but a long, thick one. This is all well and good. It is right to provide for your family. It is absolutely clear in Scripture as well, that taking care of your family has to be a top priority.

"Make it your ambition to lead a quiet life: You should mind your own business and work with your hands, just as we told you."—1 Thessalonians 4:11

"For even when we were with you, we gave you this rule: 'The one who is unwilling to work shall not eat.'"—2 Thessalonians 3:10

"Go to the ant, you sluggard; consider its ways and be wise! It has no commander, no overseer or ruler, yet it stores its provisions in summer and gathers its food at harvest."—Proverbs 6:6–8

When midlife comes around, you want to see yourself and be seen by others with a deeper significance.

associated with work, not to add to them.

As a young man, whatever the job was, it was no problem. You were willing to do it. You were out to please your boss the way you went about trying to please your parents when you lived at home.

With your first real job, whether it was related to your degree or not, came money. *Money!*

- Your paychecks were earned and you were able to spend them as you pleased.

- Along with money came more responsibility at work.

- You began to see yourself through the lens of what you did.

At your ten-year class reunion, you told others:

- I'm in sales.

- I'm in customer service.

- I'm a truck driver.

- I do computer programing for a huge firm in Silicon Valley.

You defined yourself by what you did for work. And what you did for work indicated how much money you made, either to your pride or chagrin. Our jobs meant so much to us that we simply couldn't help being defined by them.

And then came your middle years. You look up and around at your career, and begin making decisions based less on prestige and money and more on how you are valued. That may be a key to answering the big question:

Where am I going?

Once you say good riddance to defining yourself by position and title—say goodbye to that which will thwart thriving—then you are ready for this second thing you should say good riddance to:

2 Staying Involved with Workplace Drama

Especially early in a career, drama comes with the territory. Everyone in the building is defining who they are by their position and title. As a result, there is a lot of jockeying going on, a lot of gossip, a lot of people driving each other crazy.

By midlife, haven't you put in your time with this? What's it been, twenty or thirty years? It's time to retire from at least that part of your work. Plus, having had years of experience, you know what nonsense it is. Hopefully, you've found ways around it. If not, begin walking away from it little step by little step and reap the benefits of just doing the work you need to do. Then go on to enjoy your life.

But if you have a desire to stay involved in workplace drama, you will reduce the joys of however many more years of work remain for you.

PROVIDER: THINGS THAT INSPIRE THRIVING

1 You Have The "Work" Thing Down

You've been through triumphs and disasters. You've had to start over at your beginnings. And if everything around your career collapsed today, you, Provider Man, would be able to thrive again because you know how to work. You've rolled up your sleeves and gotten to work before and you can do it again. It is that basic to thriving.

- You needed extra money for Christmas one year. Or . . .

- You needed a new family vehicle. Or . . .

- You had an emergency medical bill to get off your credit card.

Remember what you did? You got to work!

In no way does this discredit the truth that God takes care of us. He took care of you by giving you the ability and understanding and knowledge to go to work. If by chance you are mentoring younger men, would you impress upon them this truth?

The world can sure be a rough place to work.

But heck, you know that. Big deal. With the way you know how to work? And with God on your side? Please! During your middle years, you should strap one hand behind your back when walking

The desire to be a good provider drives a man to excel. As a result, you have probably thrived as a Provider on many occasions.

- Did you enjoy the climb?
- Did you stumble or fall?
- Did you encounter bad climates?
- How many setbacks?

Rudyard Kipling wrote a poignant poem titled, *If*, which has a few lines that I'd like to share here: [3]

> If you can meet with Triumph and Disaster
> And treat those two impostors just the same...
> If you can make one heap of all your winnings
> And risk it on one turn of pitch-and-toss,
> And lose, and start again at your beginnings,
> And never breathe a word about your loss...
> Yours is the Earth and everything that's in it
> And—which is more—you'll be a Man,
> my son!

Those lines are just snippets of the greater work. But what I've tried to pull out is the first way that you, Man, as Provider, will be inspired to thrive.

out the door, just to keep things fair between the world and you.

2 You Understand True Teamwork

Mr. Provider,

Thank you for taking care of your family, giving to your church, caring for others in the community, and for everything you do. You have truly thrived.

Would you tell me how you did it?

Sincerely,
   Young Provider

Wouldn't that be a novel email to receive? I know what you would say and what you wouldn't say. I know you wouldn't say, "Go it alone, young man, there is no other way." Rather, what you'd say is:

- You'll need to work as a team.

- Learn to understand your coworkers.

- Be respectful of others.

- Know the value of listening to others.

- Cultivate a team environment every chance you have.

- Humbly ask for help from others.

- Express gratitude.

And you would close your reply by saying:

Don't be like me when I was your age, starting out in my career. I was brash and arrogant. I knew it all. I needed no one. Then I realized I needed my wife, and I needed my children, and I needed my church family. Finally, I realized I needed my coworkers if I was going to thrive.

Best,
   Mr. Provider
   Thriving Corporation

3 You HAVE Provided

You did it! Or, you're doing it!

Either way, what a triumph. You have provided for the basic needs of your family. You fed them, clothed them, housed them, and gave them security. This, gentlemen, is great inspiration.

Take some time to reflect on how your hard work has provided for your family. Not with the intention of going home and extolling your greatness, but just for your own mental and emotional health.

As you trudge off to the daily grind, please never forget how your effort and dedication have sustained you and your family.

Sustainable is one of our culture's catch words. You may have heard it coupled up with *agriculture, freedom, environment*, and other important values. But how about "Sustainable Family?"

Take some time to reflect on how your hard work has provided for your family.

You did it by your work; you sustained your family. Keep on keeping on! Be encouraged. Be inspired. Thrive in your provisioning!

OUR LESSON FROM BEING A PROVIDER

Now then, you know you've done a great job being a Provider. What could be the big takeaway? It is **FAITHFULNESS**.

- God has provided. He is faithful.

- You have provided. You are faithful.

- God will always provide.

Do you believe this?

- You may be facing a career or job change and you know what you want to do. But you may not know what you want to do and still want out of what you're presently doing.

- Another scenario is you really like your job but you sense you're about to get squeezed out of it.

Do you believe in the faithfulness of God? Holding onto your conviction that God is always faithful is paramount during these midlife scenarios.

Take up the task of working intentionally on one or two things at work that really need your attention. Go master those things with intentionality. See if what you're experiencing at work doesn't change as a result of your extra attention and devotion to a couple of things.

Also build your worth by thoroughly preparing anything you are asked to do. In other words, apply yourself to the work

"For we live by faith, not by sight."
—2 Corinthians 5:7

required of you like you haven't in a long, long time. Your company may suddenly realize you are undervalued—and maybe even underpaid.

Then, always remember that you are loved by the most important people: Your wife and your God. The three of you make a formidable team. That should give you confidence.

5

Father

The fifth primary role you fill during your lifetime is that of being a father. Here again, not all of you will experience fatherhood. What's significant is that, for those of you who are fathers, the utmost responsibility of raising kids sits on your shoulders. If someone calls you dad, you possess a calling of the highest order.

And then, as soon as you think you fully grasp that high calling, it seems like it is over. Those "little treasures" became "young people" and then "young adults" and suddenly they are "adults"— all grown up with careers, spouses, and kids of their own. And you wonder where that great mystery time went.

The kids that call you *Dad* do so through email, text, and other remote technological means. Rarely is the ancient phone conversation used. Promises of "seeing you soon" and "getting together soon" are tossed your way, but seldom fulfilled. School, jobs, family, are a few things that get in the middle for them.

But for you the middle is wide open. There is a gap so wide that a cruise ship can spend seven days circling it. And let's not lie to each other; the middle-aged father spends at least a few tears over this life change.

If someone calls you dad, you possess a calling of the highest order.

FATHER: THINGS THAT THWART THRIVING

Being a dad is an unending job. It is a *labor* of love, with the emphasis on labor. And if you're not Super-Dad like the guy down the street (or your brother), then the burden of the work seems to mean nothing. As a consequence, you feel like a failure time and again.

1 Dwell on How Much You Were Needed

Another way to say this could be, to find yourself longing for the old days when your family needed your help in so many ways.

Raising your babies and toddlers took a ton of work. (And your wife carried the other ten tons—let's just be honest here.) Then, once the kids were in school, it momentarily seemed like the load got lighter. Then the homework started coming and all those spelling words! Sheesh, those made you wish for a week of sleepless nights and changing diapers. (English, what a language!)

The thing is you were needed and now you're seldom called on for anything—not even advice.

The tendency is to look back with blind nostalgia on "the good old days" when you were in demand and wish for those times to come back.

> *"Start children off on the way they should go, and even when they are old they will not turn from it."*
> —Proverbs 22:6

To thrive in midlife, understand how special those years were, treasure them in your heart, but then find creative ways to form new memories with your kids during this new season.

2 Never Be Vulnerable with Your Kids

When your little rascals were growing up they saw you as Superman. You had the answers to their biggest questions:

- Dad, what's the name of that animal?

- What sound does an elephant make?

- How long before Christmas?

- Why is Billy's dad not coaching us?

And the list goes on. You had it all. You knew it all. And, well, that made you feel pretty darn good.

The questions changed over time. Did you try to answer some of them with object authority? Did you ever not know an answer but made one up anyhow? In other words, do you still try to be the superhero?

To never be vulnerable with your kids is a mistake.

I hope not. It will thwart thriving because your kids are older and wiser now. They will find you out, and maybe even call you out, if you try to bluff your way with them. That will cause a rift in the relationship you just don't want to have to try and repair.

To never be vulnerable with your kids is a mistake. It doesn't matter what age they are—child or teenager or adult.

- When you don't have the answers to a specific question or challenge, tell them you don't. And then work with your child to find those answers.

- Let them see you are a real person with limited understanding.

- Be a dad that doesn't have to know everything.

Do these simple things and you'll be a dad your children respect and admire for his humility and vulnerability.

3 Being Unapologetic

- Have you let your children down?

- Have you hurt your children in some way?

It is part of being a father. You and I—and the entire gender—are flawed men. We first of all need the help of the Lord Jesus to rescue us from our sinful nature and transform us into new creatures. We so badly need the grace of God to cover us as we father that I cannot express how truly needy we are.

Without Jesus' forgiveness, we fathers will never get things right. We just can't do it. Being "Dad" is too much for a man without God.

In middle age, we begin to realize that we may have screwed up some things with our children. We may also realize that we need to address our screw-ups by seeking forgiveness.

Being "Dad" is too much for a man without God.

Are you holding on to baggage like this? Don't prolong being unapologetic. The longer you carry baggage the heavier it gets. Go and apologize to your children. Seek forgiveness. There is no shame in humbling yourself before children you have hurt.

To thrive, do everything you can to make your relationship with your children right.

- Be humble.

- Talk to them.

- Listen to them.

- Get everything out in the open.

- Take responsibility.

- Ask for their forgiveness.

- Be hopeful.

The best part is God wants this for you. He is on your side in the task to keep the harboring of unforgiveness away. He knows it will thwart your midlife. God is the ultimate forgiver, so he will equip you for the journey.

FATHER: THINGS THAT INSPIRE THRIVING

1 Knowing You Did Your Job

The heading pretty much says it all: You know in your heart of hearts that you fathered the best you could, moment by moment of every day.

With this knowledge, and any baggage dealt with already, you are encouraged to jump into midlife with the freedom of a skydiver. You don't have to try to recompense anything or anyone anymore. You went through the tough times and easier times like a champ. You have a right to stand proud in the center of your life knowing you fought the good fight of fathering.

Congratulations, Dad!

2 You've Learned to Love and Be Loved

You should be inspired to thrive with knowing this. I think all of us men thought we knew everything there was to know about love before we were fathers. But it actually took a screaming baby, years of discipline, sibling and friend drama, and a host of other experiences as a father to really learn the true nature of love.

Did you ever think you could receive such unconditional love and affection from another human?

Like what we knew about the love of God: "God is love" (1 John 4:8).

We thought we understood God. Then he gave us children and from day one, if not before, we learned about setting ourselves aside for the sake of our baby. We could have ignored the cries and the diapers and the baths. We could have contracted our work to the lowest bidder. But no, we did what God did for us; we loved and lived and gave ourselves in every way to our children. So we learned something more about God's love: Sacrifice really meant death to self.

> "For God so loved the world that he gave his one and only Son, that whoever believes in him shall not perish but have eternal life."
> —John 3:16

And on the receiving side of love, my goodness, did you ever think you could receive such unconditional love and affection from another human? Those kids of ours have no pretense about pouring out themselves to please us. We don't push them away, ignore their hugs and cuddles, or dismiss their efforts at affection. We got loved by our children who seemingly knew more about true love than we did. Dads really are blessed beyond measure.

The fact that you have learned to love and be loved bodes well for you in the future. Cling to what you've learned from your children about love and you'll thrive in midlife and beyond.

3 Appreciating Your Own Parents More

How many times did you think of your parents while you faced being a parent? How many situations did you face that made you appreciate your parents more then you did before?

If you are anything like this dad, there have been many times. I'll tell you, I had no idea how much my mom and dad did for me until I had to do so much for my children. I'm not even talking about the feeding and changing anymore. I'm talking about the struggle to figure out the bedtime routine or how to best discipline that little girl that disobeys and then smiles so adorably.

However, did my mom and dad deal with . . . well, deal with me?

Our children are an amazing blessing to us. It takes looking back on those amazing blessings from the vantage point of midlife for us to realize how much of a blessing our parents were to us, too.

Gentlemen, God is so good to us. Do you realize this? I hope and pray you do. If you aren't a father yet, or never will be, but your dad is still living, would you embrace him as soon as you can? Tell him what a blessing he is. If your father has passed away, you can still write him a letter thanking him for his sacrifice on your behalf. Just file it away.

I believe if men like ourselves:

- Would just rejoice a little more about fatherhood

- Grieve a little more if need be

- Reach out to fatherless boys

- Embrace an old man who doesn't have children

Well, then our entire gender, from the youngest to the oldest would quit hurting so much. I think men would finally be more Christ-like.

Before moving on to the lesson learned from being a father, would you receive this benediction from Jude 24–25? Gentlemen, fathers, dads, be blessed as you have been a blessing:

> To him who is able to keep you from stumbling and to present you before his glorious presence without fault and with great joy—to the only God our Savior be glory, majesty, power and authority, through Jesus Christ our Lord, before all ages, now and forevermore! Amen.

OUR LESSON FROM BEING A FATHER

The reason I closed the above section with that beautiful benediction is because the words, if you read them thoughtfully, express everything a man could ever want from a blessing. Read it again. It will humble you.

The big takeaway from being a father is
HUMILITY.

Fatherhood invites us to be humble.

I look at that Jude passage and when I read, "to
make you stand" I get to thinking about how I
must not have been standing otherwise. If God is
going to make us stand in the presence of his glory
"without fault and with great joy" it must be that
we weren't standing before. Which means I must
have been on my knees or prostrate.

And then I realize that's how I should be before
God—in a posture of humility.

Fatherhood invites us to be humble. *Invites* may be the wrong word, because I think God planned it for us. But I guess we could reject his plan, so maybe *invites* is appropriate.

At the time we have a child, we're fairly certain we have the raising of that child in our control. Sure, we say the child is a gift of God and so on; but really, we mean we've got this from here, God. Thank you for the gift.

However, in God's perfect plan, our kids grow up. And pretty soon, when they are smarter and bigger and stronger, they find their independence. We fathers all of a sudden matter less, and, indeed, have less control.

Enter humility.

I like to explain this process of attaining humility like this:

> As fathers, we are so tempted to think of ourselves as absolutely powerful. Bit by bit, our children teach us how little power we have. If one of God's purposes is to teach us humility, then in the process of parenting, he sure did come up with a great plan.[4]

What we thought we had, power, we realize we never really had. It was ourselves that were actually codependent with God, not raising the child on our own at all. Our children were God's design from before the foundation of the world (Ephesians 1:4), and for several years we forgot that "little" bit of truth.

In midlife, you will thrive with true humility developed in your character. It took several years after becoming a father to develop that humility, but now that you've embraced it, can you drop to your knees in gratitude?

Remember, God will make you stand when his plan for you is to make you stand.

— 6 —

Man of God

What do I mean by *Man of God*? I mean:

- A man who lets Scripture inform his life and how to live.

- A man who pursues righteousness and fights the good fight of faith.

- A man who won't compromise and won't take credit that belongs to God.

- A man who willingly sets aside his own will for the benefit of others.

You know what? You are prepared to be the man of God I'm talking about. The first half of your life has prepared you to be a man of God. If you think again about the five big takeaways that God has taught you from the roles you play, you'll realize how ingrained they are in your character.

Be this kind of man and thrive. Be this kind of man and you'll be a man of God.

JUST ONE MORE

The Bible tells us a very intriguing quality about a certain man. This quality was such a significant part of this man's character that his friends changed his name to reflect this quality, which flowed from his heart.

You are prepared to be the man of God I'm talking about.

This man actually sold a piece of property and brought the money to the apostles for them to use to benefit others.

Have you picked up on who this man is? It is Barnabas: "Joseph, a Levite from Cyprus, whom the apostles called Barnabas (which means "son of encouragement"), sold a field he owned and brought the money and put it at the apostles' feet" (Acts 4:36–37).

The quality of a Man of God I'm adding here is **ENCOURAGEMENT**.

A man in his middle years has a unique set of gifts, which we've seen in several ways above.

- You are gifted with wisdom, so encourage those who aren't.

- You are gifted with status, position, title, so encourage those who are without rank.

■ You are gifted with possessions, so use them to encourage those who go without.

The list of your gifts is for you to continue. I encourage you to do so. And then, by all means, go and be a Barnabas to someone. As an encourager, you will surely thrive.

MAN OF GOD: THINGS THAT INSPIRE THRIVING

1 A man who lets scripture inform his life.

"All Scripture is God-breathed and is useful for teaching, rebuking, correcting and training in righteousness, so that the servant of God may be thoroughly equipped for every good work."
—2 Timothy 3:16–17

You are equipped for every good work you will do during your middle years and into your golden years. You are adequate. And the more time you spend studying the scriptures the better off you'll be. The man of God takes the scriptures seriously. It doesn't mean he has to go out and preach from rooftops. But it does mean he has the answers he needs when he needs them.

2 A man who pursues righteousness and fights the good fight of faith.

"But you, man of God, flee from all this, and pursue righteousness, godliness, faith, love, endurance and gentleness. Fight the good fight of the faith. Take hold of the eternal life to which you were called when you made your good confession in the presence of many witnesses."
—1 Timothy 6:11–12

You are equipped for every good work you will do during your middle years and into your golden years.

You are in prime position to live out this passage of scripture. First of all, you are already in the pursuit of righteousness and the others. Secondly, you've been in the good fight of the faith for many years. Midlife simply offers you another season by which you can go to battle. Continue to fight against sin. And continue to fight for that which is virtuous.

3 A man who won't compromise and won't take credit that belongs to God.

"When Elisha the man of God heard that the king of Israel had torn his robes, he sent him this message: 'Why have you torn your robes? Have the man come to me and he will know that there is a prophet in Israel.'

"Then Naaman and all his attendants went back to the man of God. He stood before him and said, 'Now I know that there is no God in all the world except in Israel. So please accept a gift from your servant.'

"The prophet answered, 'As surely as the LORD lives, whom I serve, I will not accept a thing.' And even though Naaman urged him, he refused."
—2 Kings 5:8,15–16

Like Elisha, a man of God doesn't do anything that misrepresents his God.

You have the privilege to be a voice of reason and wisdom to others, especially the next generation. You may also find you are in a place of power that allows you to dictate the comings and goings of others. You could also be in a position where taking a little on the side would benefit you. But like Elisha, a man of God doesn't do anything that misrepresents his God. If God performs a mighty deed, you aren't there taking the credit.

There are plenty of men who will want the credit. But not the man of God.

4 A man who willingly sets aside his own will for the benefit of others.

"Therefore, I urge you, brothers and sisters, in view of God's mercy, to offer your bodies as a living sacrifice, holy and pleasing to God—this is your true and proper worship. Do not conform to the pattern of this world, but be transformed by the renewing of your mind. Then you will be able to test and approve what God's will is—his good, pleasing and perfect will."—Romans 12:1–2

You have heard this passage a thousand times. And still it is worth another meditation. Jesus Christ is the exemplar here and so the man of God will desire to be like Christ.

The passage keys on the "Do not conform to the pattern of this world" and it is because that is so difficult to do. Even for a man who has matured and grown in grace and knowledge of the Lord, the world, like the harlot of Proverbs (7:10–23), calls aloud, beckons in every possible way for a man to conform to her ways.

One of the insights into this passage reveals how the appeal is for your body, spirit, mind, and will to all be involved. And so we have an echo of our Lord's words: "Love the Lord your God with all your heart and with all your soul and with all your mind and with all your strength" (Mark 12:30).

As a man of God, you understand this and passionately pursue such an end.

Conclusion

I pray that you will benefit from what you discovered in this book. You have ongoing purpose as:

- Macho Man
- Son
- Husband
- Provider
- Father
- Man of God

Thriving isn't a right, but a pursuit.

- What joys and rejoicing you will find.
- What love for your wife you will have.
- What an understanding of your children you will possess.

May God richly bless you!

Notes

1. Stephen Arterburn and John Shore, *Midlife Manual for Men: Finding Significance in The Second Half*, (Minneapolis, Minnesota: Bethany House Pub., 2008), 37.

2. Ibid., 119.

3. Rudyard Kipling, "If," *Rewards and Fairies*. https://en.wikipedia.org/wiki/If%E2%80%94 (accessed April 11, 2017).

4. Arterburn and Shore, *Midlife Manual for Men: Finding Significance in The Second Half*, 176.

OTHER RESOURCES FROM STEPHEN ARTERBURN

7 WAYS TO CHOOSE HEALING
Learn how to make choices to ensure you experience the healing God, in his eternal purpose, has for you.
Paperback, 124 pages, 4.5 x 6.5

ISBN: 9781628624298 | PRODUCT CODE: 4139X

6 WAYS FOR MEN TO THRIVE IN MIDLIFE
Midlife doesn't have to be a crisis of identity or a failure in self-confidence. Midlife can be a season of discovering how your past years and present situation are the very material to make an exciting future.
Paperback, 124 pages, 4.5 x 6.5

ISBN: 9781628624489 | PRODUCT CODE: 4149X

5 WAYS TO OVERCOME TOXIC FAITH
Toxic faith replaces a person's relationship with God with a religious practice. If you are concerned that you or someone you love may be involved in a toxic church or organization, this book offers real hope.
Paperback, 124 pages, 4.5 x 6.5

ISBN: 9781628624502 | PRODUCT CODE: 4151X

NEW LIFE MINISTRIES, founded by Steve Arterburn, exists to go into life's hardest places with you. Visit NewLife.com today to see how we can help. Be sure to check our live call-in times for New Life Live!, or call 800-HELP-4-ME to hear the next available time. We want to hear from you!

www.hendricksonrose.com
www.aspirepress.com